NEWFOUNDLANDS

by Allan Morey

Content Consultant: Sarah K. Crain
Doctor of Veterinary Medicine
Tufts University
North Grafton, Massachusetts

Pebble® Plus

CAPSTONE PRESS
a capstone imprint

Pebble Plus is published by Capstone Press,
1710 Roe Crest Drive, North Mankato, Minnesota 56003
www.mycapstone.com

Library of Congress Cataloging-in-Publication Data
Morey, Allan, author.
Newfoundlands / by Allan Morey.
    pages cm. -- (Big dogs)
Audience: Ages 5-7.
Audience: K to grade 3.
Summary: "Simple text and full-color photographs describe
Newfoundlands"-- Provided by publisher.
Includes bibliographical references and index.
ISBN 978-1-4914-7980-3 (library binding)
ISBN 978-1-4914-8564-4 (ebook PDF)
1. Newfoundland dog--Juvenile literature. 2. Dog breeds--Juvenile
literature. I. Title.
SF429.N4M67 2016
636.73--dc23   2015030282

Editorial Credits
Nikki Bruno Clapper, editor; Juliette Peters, designer;
Morgan Walters, media researcher; Katy LaVigne, production specialist

Photo Credits
Glow Images: Juniors Bildarchiv, 9; iStockphoto: JudiLen, 7; Newscom: SHANNON STAPLETON,
19, WOLFGANG RATTAY, 17; Shutterstock: andrewvec, (speedometer) cover, Charles T. Bennett,
15, cynoclub, 5, Eric Isselee, (dog) bottom left 22, Ermolaev Alexander, cover, Hywit Dimyadi, (dog
silhouette) cover, kostolom3000, (dog head) backcover, 3, Ksenia Raykova, 1, Liliya Kulianionak, 11,
Lukas Hejtman, 13, Stephaniellen, (elephant) bottom right 22, vlastas, (paw prints) design element
throughout, Yan Zommer, 21; Wikimedia: Bobby Mikul, 7

Note to Parents and Teachers

The Big Dogs set supports national science standards related to life science. This book describes
and illustrates Newfoundlands. The images support early readers in understanding the text. The
repetition of words and phrases helps early readers learn new words. This book also introduces
early readers to subject-specific vocabulary words, which are defined in the Glossary section. Early
readers may need assistance to read some words and to use the Table of Contents, Glossary, Read
More, Internet Sites, Critical Thinking Using the Common Core, and Index sections of the book.

Printed in the United States of America in North Mankato, Minnesota.
102015   009221CGS16

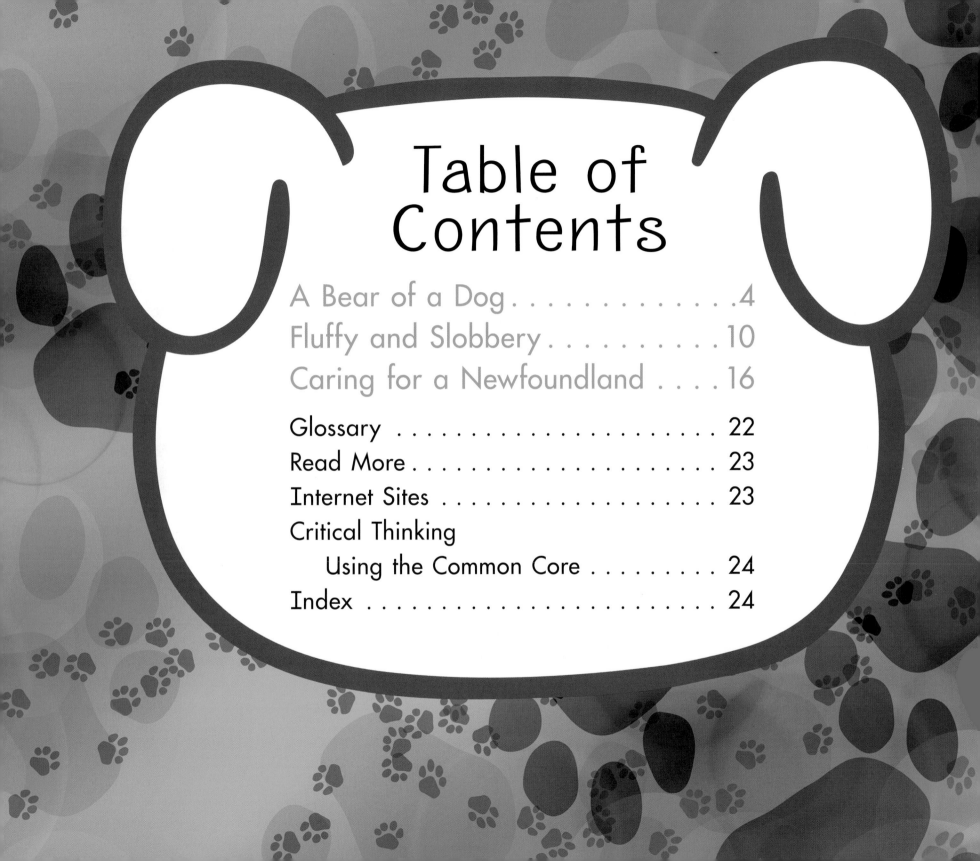

Table of Contents

A BEAR OF A DOG

Bear would be a great

name for a Newfoundland.

They are big dogs with

shaggy hair like a bear's.

Say It Like This:
NEW-fuhnd-lend

Newfoundlands are called
working dogs. People train
them for water rescues.
These great swimmers even
have webbed feet!

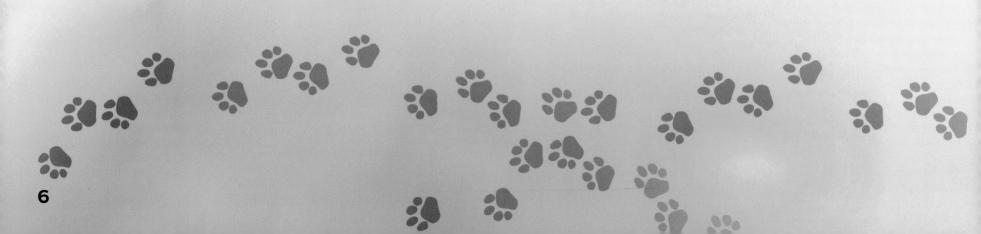

Owners of Newfoundlands
call them Newfies for short.
Newfies are big, strong,
and loving. They are good
with kids and other pets.

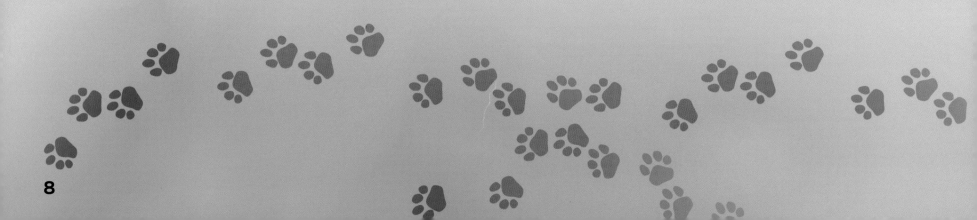

FLUFFY AND SLOBBERY

The thick coat of a Newfie has two layers. The under layer is soft. The outer layer is rough. A Newfie's coat resists water.

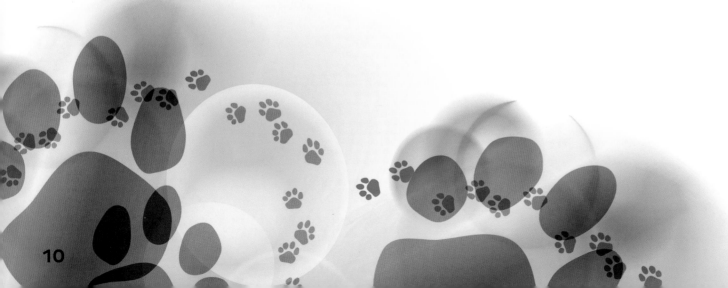

Newfies are droolers. When
they shake their huge heads,
slobber flies everywhere.
Newfie owners must be ready
to wipe up slobber!

Newfies are sweet, playful pets. They are loyal to their families. These big dogs live for 8 to 10 years.

CARING FOR A NEWFOUNDLAND

Newfies need good training.

They are so strong they can

drag you around on walks.

They are so big they can

knock people over!

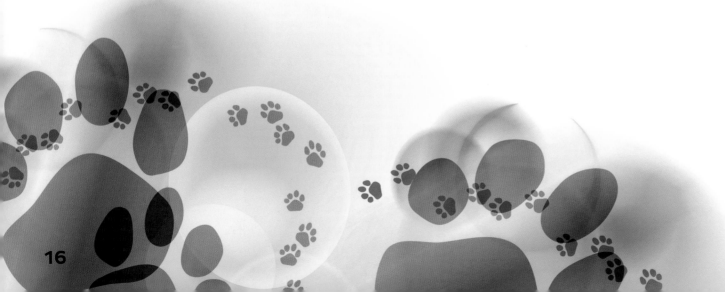

Newfies' coats need a lot
of care. They need to be
brushed a couple of times
each week. They also shed.
A vacuum cleaner is a must!

Newfies need care
and attention. But they
give back lots of love.
These huggable dogs want
to be your best friend.

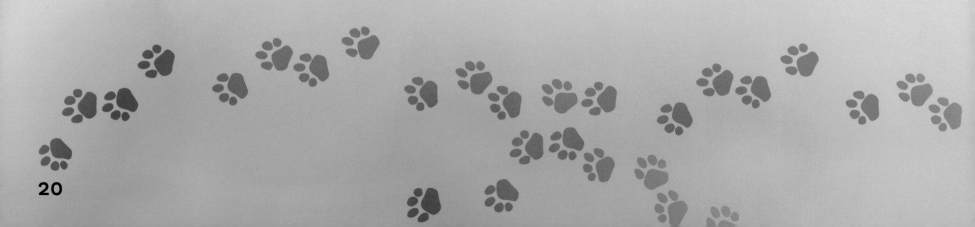

GLOSSARY

coat—an animal's hair or fur

drool—spit that drips from the mouth

loyal—being true to something or someone

rescue—to save someone who is in danger

resist—to keep away

shaggy—long and rough, like shaggy hair

shed—to drop or fall off; some dogs shed their hair

training—teaching an animal to do what you say

webbed—having folded skin or tissue between an animal's toes or fingers; webbed feet help animals swim

working dog—a dog that is bred to do a job, such as rescuing people or guarding homes

HOW BIG ARE THEY?

	Newfoundland	Baby Elephant
Average Height	26–30 inches (66–76 centimeters)	36 inches (91 cm)
Average Weight	100–150 pounds (45–68 kilograms)	200 pounds (91 kg)

READ MORE

Green, Sara. *Water Rescue Dogs.* Pilot: Dogs to the Rescue! Minneapolis, Minn.: Bellwether Media, 2014.

Hutmacher, Kimberly M. *I Want a Dog.* I Want a Pet. Mankato, Minn.: Capstone Press, 2012.

Landau, Elaine. *Newfoundlands Are the Best!* Best Dogs Ever. Minneapolis, Minn.: Lerner, 2011.

INTERNET SITES

FactHound offers a safe, fun way to find Internet sites related to this book. All of the sites on FactHound have been researched by our staff.

Here's all you do:

Visit *www.facthound.com*

Type in this code: 9781491479803

 **Super-cool stuff!** Check out projects, games and lots more at **www.capstonekids.com**

CRITICAL THINKING
USING THE COMMON CORE

1. What features of Newfoundlands make them good rescue dogs?
   (Key Ideas and Details)

2. Do you think you would be able to take care of a pet Newfoundland?
   What would be the hardest part?
   (Integration of Knowledge and Ideas)

INDEX